I'll Talk to God About That

Dandi Daley Mackall

Illustrated by Janet Samuel

HARVEST HOUSE PUBLISHERS
EUGENE, OREGON

To Ellie Hendren
–Dandi Daley Mackall

To Alice
–Janet Samuel

I'll Talk to God About That

Text copyright © 2014 by Dandi Daley Mackall
Artwork copyright © 2014 by Janet Samuel

Published by Harvest House Publishers
Eugene, Oregon 97402
www.harvesthousepublishers.com

ISBN 978-0-7369-5875-2

Design and production by Mary pat Design, Westport, Connecticut

Printed in China

14 15 16 17 18 19 20 21 / LP / 10 9 8 7 6 5 4 3 2 1

[Jesus said:]
"I am leaving you with a gift—
peace of mind and heart.
And the peace I give is a gift the
world cannot give. So don't be
troubled or afraid."

John 14:27

Fear of Monsters

and the Unknown

When I'm face-to-face with a huge giraffe,
And his neck's as long as a shepherd's staff

I can feel the fear, but I'll choose to laugh.
And I'll talk to God about that.

Fear of the Dark

Bedtime, and Thunder

When it's dark at night, I'm alone in bed.
Then the thunder booms! I could hide my head.

But I'll think of God, and I'll pray instead.
And I'll talk to God about that.

Fear of Separation

When my mommy leaves and I have to stay,
I could fuss and cry, but it doesn't pay.

She will come back home to me anyway.
And I'll talk to God about that.

Fear of Getting Los

nd Being Alone

If I think I'm lost in the shopping mall,
And the crowd is big but I'm pretty small,

I will stop and pray. I know Who to call.
And I'll talk to God about that.

Fear of the

Unfamiliar

In a brand new place, when it's up to me,
I can talk to God very quietly.

Then I'll do my best. For the rest, we'll see...
'Cause I'll talk to God about that.

As I grow and grow, I can face all fear.

I'll be worry-free

'cause I know God's near.

If I feel afraid, then I'll give this cheer:

God, I'll talk to You about that!

Other scary things I can talk to God about:

_____

_____

_____

_____

_____

Scriptures

Where God's love is, there is no fear, because God's perfect love drives out fear.
1 John 4:18 NCV

Look at the birds in the air. They don't plant or harvest or store food in barns, but your heavenly Father feeds them. And you know that you are worth much more than the birds.
Matthew 6:26 NCV

I will not be afraid, because the Lord is my helper. People can't do anything to me.
Hebrews 13:6 NCV

For you are my hiding place; you protect me from trouble.
Psalm 32:7

I will not be afraid,
for you are close beside me.
Psalm 23:4

Give your worries to the LORD,
and he will take care of you.
Psalm 55:22 NCV

When they call on me, I will answer;
I will be with them in trouble.
I will rescue and honor them.
Psalm 91:15

I will be your God throughout your lifetime—
until your hair is white with age.
I made you, and I will care for you.
I will carry you along and save you.
Isaiah 46:4

Thank You, God,
for letting me talk to
You about everything.
I'm tossing my fears
up to You.
Thanks for loving me.
I love You too!
Amen.